NOMEN HERBAE ROSMARINI

The Herbal of Apuleius. Dioscorides and Apuleius,
sixth/seventh century

ALSO IN THIS SERIES FROM THE HERB SOCIETY:

In Praise of Parsley

A Multitude of Mints

In Celebration of Chives

The Romance of Rosemary

Compiled by Guy Cooper & Gordon Taylor

Preface by Caroline Conran

THE HERB SOCIETY
in association with
THE JUNIPER PRESS

**To
"my mother"
Jane Cooper**

© The Herb Society & The Juniper Press 1981

All Rights Reserved.
No Part of this publication may be reproduced, stored in a retrieval system, or transmitted, in any form or by any means, electronic, mechanical, photocopying, recording, or otherwise without the written permission of the publishers.

ISBN 0 903981 39 4
ISBN 0 906390 07 9

First published in Great Britain, 1981 by
The Herb Society, London & The Juniper Press, Winchester.
Cover designed by Terry Stratton
Illustrations: "By courtesy of the Wellcome Trustees"
Printed in Great Britain by Gabare Ltd., London & Winchester
 in Linoterm Plantin on Longbow Cartridge.

'Seethe much Rosemary, and bathe therein to make thee lusty, lively, joyfull, likeing and youngly.'

THE GARDEN OF HEALTH
William Langham, 1579

ROSMARINO SILVESTRE

The *Herbario Nuovo* of Castore Durante. Rome, 1585

Preface

Rosemary, more than most herbs, is delicious to grow. Not because it is serviceable, like parsley, but because it is truly a romantic and beautiful plant, as you will find from reading this little book.

Gertrude Jekyll writes in her *House and Garden* of planting 'ever-blessed rosemary all over the garden, so that at every few steps the passer-by can run his hand over the blue-flowered branchlets and smell the warm resinous, incense in his palm'.

In actual fact, rosemary is as common as brambles in many parts of the Mediterranean, but for some reason not often appreciated by cooks as warmly as it is by gardeners. However, one is very likely to detect the smell of rosemary and garlic, with which it has a particular affinity since the garlic tempers the strong flavour of the herb, in almost any kitchen where there is an Italian at work. It is a basic Tuscan herb, and there is currently a strong interest in the cooking of Tuscany which is considered healthful and wholesome both in Italy and in the newly-enthusiastic Britain and United States, who seem to have discovered only recently that Italians don't live just on spaghetti bolognese.

Italians certainly love rosemary best in the kitchen, using it in sprigs with unpeeled cloves of garlic – not just one but several if possible – under every piece of roast pork, veal, lamb, with rabbit, inside chickens and fish, and even in bread. Panini de rosmarino, rosemary bread, was once associated with the Thursday of Easter week – in the same sort of way that we associate hot cross buns with Good Friday. This bread, containing rosemary and olive oil, was sold outside churches to the devout, whose appetite-rousing duty it was on that particular day to visit seven churches, one after the other.

The trouble with rosemary, if it has a trouble, is that it tends to be all-powerful and too pervasive – in fact at one time when a good deal of cooking was done in quantities of lard, if the lard smelled too reminiscent of the pig-sty, branches of rosemary were heated in it to overpower and replace the smell of swine. And, if a room smells musty or foul for some reason, a few branches of rosemary burned in the fireplace will fill the air with a sweet fragrance.

I love this little book, with its conjuring of old ways and myths, it's reminder of a past rich use of the English language and its evocation of even more pleasant associations for a plant that is already a favourite with most gardeners and many cooks. Like the herb, the book, which is practical as well as romantic, 'gladdeth and lighteth alle men that use it'.

Caroline Conran

A Curious Herbal. Elizabeth Blackwell. London, 1798

Rosemary
Rosmarinus officinalis – Linnaeus

Latin derivation:
ros = dew; marinus = sea

Dew of the Sea

Family: *Labiatae*

Height: up to 6 feet
1200-1500 mm

Flowers: April/May
August/September

Hardy Evergreen Shrub

Synonyms: Polar Plant
Compass Weed
Compass Plant
Early French Incensier
French Romarin
German Rosmarein
Italian Rosmarino
Spanish Romero Rosmario
Portuguese Alecrim
Dutch Rosemarijn
Arabic Ikil-Jabal

Habitat: Rosemary is native to southern Europe, Asia Minor, and along the Mediterranean coasts from the Balkan Peninsula to Spain and

Portugal, though only in isolated areas in Turkey, the Lebanon and Egypt; it grows best by the sea but will grow inland and is found even in regions of the Sahara. Rosemary has been cultivated in Great Britain for over six hundred years. Some sources say it was one of the herbs probably brought here by the Romans, then went out of cultivation until the fourteenth century when it was re-introduced by Queen Phillipa, wife to King Edward III.

Some other Varieties:
Rosmarinus officinalis albus
    White flower/quite rare
Rosmarinus officinalis argenteus
    silver variegated leaf/rare
Rosmarinus officinalis aureus
    golden variegated leaf/half-hardy
Rosmarinus officinalis 'Benenden Blue'
    bright blue flower
Rosmarinus officinalis fastigiatus
    'Miss Jessop's Upright/erect
Rosmarinus officinalis prostratus*
    dense low-growing mats/tender
Rosmarinus officinalis roseus
    pink flower
Rosmarinus officinalis 'Severn Sea'
    brilliant blue flower

---

* now named Rosemary lavandulaceus

CULTIVATION: The common rosemary is a dense, fragrant, evergreen shrub with linear, spiky leaves, greyish-green above and downy-white beneath. It has clusters of double-lipped pale blue flowers which are much loved by bees. It is a very aromatic plant and the taste is camphorous and on a hot day the fragrance is of pine needles.

The herb does best in light, rather dry soil, and with some shelter from winter winds, but it will grow in any type of well-drained limey soil. In northern climates or where soil is badly drained it is best to grow rosemary in a pot drained with broken crocks near a south or west-facing wall and over-winter it in a greenhouse or indoors. It thrives in southern Britain, but must be protected from frost in northern climates such as north of England, New England and Canada.

There are three methods of propagation: seed, cuttings and layering. Growing from seed is slow. Taking cuttings in the summer of ripe terminal shoots 2 to 4 inches long or cuttings from the half-ripened wood with a 'heel' is the quickest form of increase. Layering can be done from older bushes with branches long enough to bend down and peg the into the soil, and when rooting has taken place, then the rooted section of the branch is severed from the mother plant. Layering is considered the most fool-proof form of propagation.

Indoors, rosemary can be grown successfully along with other perennial culinary herbs: chives, mint, thyme, winter savory etc. The growing situation should be south, west or even an east-facing window-sill. The room must have good air circulation and not be too humid nor too dry; if it's the latter then a bowl of water should be placed near the plants. The compost: a prepared potting mixture or good garden soil mixed with sand, should be kept moist, but not waterlogged, for death comes to herbs and other indoor plants during the winter especially by those well-intended but unnecessary long drinks of water.

Rosemary is an ideal pot plant in cold climates, particularly in North America, and if a plant is kept slightly potbound it is then encouraged to bloom. The woody nature of rosemary makes it an excellent subject for cultivation as Bonsai – specifically the prostratus form: *Rosemarinus lavandulaceus*.

> ' The gilliflower also, the skilfull do know,
> doth look to be covered in frost and in snow:
> the knot and the border, and the rosemary gay,
> do crave the like succour, for dying away.'
>
> *Five Hundreth Points of Good Husbandry*
> Thomas Tusser, 1573

Commercially, France is the main source of Rosemary.

The Keeping of Rosemary: This herb has a high degree of essential oil and it should be harvested when the flowers are in bud – the rule for harvesting most herbs – not in full flower for then the essential oil is diminished. The optimum time for harvesting on a fine sunny day is between say, 11 a.m. and 4 p.m. The leaves should be stripped from the branches, placed evenly on drying trays – simply a wood frame with muslin or netting – and put into a well-ventilated airing cupboard. If quickly dried the rosemary leaves should retain a good green colour; store in air-tight dark glass jars.

ROSMARINO.

The *Herbario Nuovo* of Castore Durante. Rome, 1585

YTH AND HISTORY: Irrespective of culture, religion or political system the ancient world used herbs primarily for their medicinal, culinary and cosmetic virtues – both real and imagined. Anthropologists and archaeologists have found evidence that herbs were used in all major ancient civilisations: Egypt; Mesopotamia; China; India; North, Middle, South America and the Mediterranean basin.

Rosemary had a reputation with the Greeks for strengthening the brain and the memory. The Romans employed it in their bath houses and as a strewing herb.

There are many Christian legends attached to rosemary: here are two. While the Virgin Mary was resting on the flight to Egypt she happened to place her cloak over a rosemary bush, and forever afterwards, the flowers which had been white turned to the heavenly blue of the garment.

A second tale is that rosemary will not grow taller than the height of the mature Jesus Christ – about six feet according to theologians – and that after 33 years (Christ's age at the crucifixion) a rosemary bush will grow in breadth but not in height.

Rosemary has played its part in fairy stories as well: this is the herb that was tried, but failed to awaken *The Sleeping Beauty*.

> 'Rosemary, "it mighteth the boones and causeth goode and gladeth and lighteth alle men that use it.

The leves layde under the head whanne a man slepes, it doth away evell spirites and suffereth not to dreame fowle dremes ne to be afeade. But he must be out of deedely synne for it is an holy tree. Lavender and Rosemary is as woman to man and Whote Roose to Reede. It is an holy tree and with ffolke that been just and Rightfull gladlye it groweth and thryveth."'

Written in the fourteenth century by the Countess of Hainault to her daughter Queen Phillipa of England, wife of Kind Edward III.

British Herbal. Sir John Hill. London, 1756

ROSEMARY AS A SYMBOL

Weddings
'As trim as a Bride's rosemary'
>Sir W. Cornwallis
>*Essays, 1601*

'Go get you in then, and let your husband dip the Rosemary'
>Killigrew
>*Parson's Wedding,* 1663

'The bride was led to church between two sweet boys with bridelaces and Rosemary tied to their silken sleeves.'
>Brand
>*Popular Antiquities,* 1777

Funerals:
'Grow if for two ends, it matters not at all,
Be't for my bridall or my buriall'
>*Robert Herrick*
>1591-1674

'Heaven and yourself had part in this fair maid: now heaven hath all, and all the better it is for the maid:
Your part in her you could not keep from death; But heaven keeps his part in eternal life.
. . . Dry up yours tears and stick your rosemary on this fair corse.'
>Friar Laurence to the Capulets
>*Romeo and Juliet,* Act iv, Scene 3.

'My body to the earth without any ceremony, then Rosemary and wine'
>*Somerset Ho*
>Will of Tooker, 1682

'Oh, thou great shepheard, Lobbin, how great is they griefe?
Where bene the nosegays she dight for thee?
  the coloured chaplets wrought with a chiefe
The knotted rush rings and gilt rosemarie?'
>November, *Shepheard's Calender*
>Edmund Spenser, 1552-1599

'There goes a funeral with the Men of Rosemary after it.'
>*T. Brown,* 1700

Remembrance and Friendship:
'For you there's rosemary and rue; these keep Seeming and savour all the winter long: Grace and remembrance be to you both.'
>Perdita
>*The Winter's Tale*, Act iv, Scene 3.
>William Shakespeare.

'As for Rosemarine, I lett it runne all over my garden walls, not onlie because by bees love it, but because it is the herb sacred to remembrance, and, therefore, to friendship; whence a sprig of it hath a dumb language that maketh it the chosen emblem of our funeral wakes and in our buriall grounds.'
>*Sir Thomas More*
>1478-1535

'There's rosemary, that's for remembrance; pray you love, remember . . .'
>Ophelia
>*Hamlet*, Act iv, Scene 5.
>William Shakespeare.

Hortus Sanitatus. Mainz, 1485

ERBALS: Because rosemary and the other common culinary herbs are indigenous to southern Europe and the Mediterranean areas, their historical importance as useful and delightful plants first emerged in the botanical works of those most important men who initially began to identify and experiment with herbs and other plants. They include Aristotle, Theophrastus, Pliny the Elder, and Dioscorides whose great illustrated work on medicinal plants 'De Materia Medica' – written in the first century – became the fundamental botanical source-work for succeeding centuries. It was copied out and translated many times by religious centres and monastic houses into Latin, Greek, Arabic and Persian. Those holy places also cultivated and conserved important herbs for about a thousand years.

In the fifth century one Apuleius Platonicus combined his own texts including medicinal recipes and plant illustrations with those of Dioscorides. Even though scholars have denigrated *The Herbal of Apuleius*, yet it is 'in its way a landmark in the history both of botany and botanical illustration. It was probably written in the south of France, and for many generations was unhappily to provide western illustrators from Italy to the Rhine with a storehouse for

19

plunder.'* Nonetheless it existed and its historical impact cannot be disregarded.

The monks at Monte Cassino wrote translations of *Apuleius* from Greek and Arabic and from that monastery came a ninth-century version, destroyed during World War II, which was the herbal model for the Anglo-Saxons. Their herbals were titled *Leech Books* for the physicians of the time rejoiced in the name of Leeches . . . The earliest of these herbals, *The Leech Book of Bald* was written in the Anglo-Saxon vernacular around the year 1000. Rosemary is listed there as a remedy for toothache; sage, garlic, leek, elecampane, hyssop, onion and betony are some other herbs mentioned.

The Herbal of Apuleius also influenced some of the earliest printed herbals made in Italy and Germany during the sixteenth century. The history of herbals and botanical illustration is complex and fascinating and we have tried to show some of that chronicle through the quotations and illustrations in this small book.

The Illustrated Herbal
Wilfrid Blunt and Sandra Raphael. Frances Lincoln. London, 1980. (An excellent book on the subject with 159 plates)

THE HERBAL OR GENERAL HISTORY
of PLANTS
John Gerard, 1597
revised by Thomas Johnson, 1633

Of Rosemarie

The Place
Rosemarie groweth in France, Spaine, and in other hot countries; in woods, and in untilled places, there is such plentie thereof in Languedock, that the inhabitants burne scarce any other fuell: they make hedges of it in the gardens of Italy and England, being a great ornament unto the name: it groweth neither in the fields nor gardens of the Easterne cold countries; but is carefully and curiously kept in pots, set into stoves and sellers, against the injuries of their cold Winters.

Wilde Rosemarie groweth in Lancashire in divers places, especially in a field called Little Reed, amongst the Hurtleberries, neere unto a small village called Maudsley; there found by a learned Gentleman often remembered in our historie (and that worthily) Mr. Thomas Hesketh.

The Time
Rosemarie floureth twice a yeare, in the Spring and after in August. The Wild Rosemarie floureth in June and July.

The Temperature
Rosemarie is hot and drie in the second degree, and also of an stringent or binding quality, as being compounded of divers parts, and taking more of the mixture of the earthy substance.

The Vertues
Rosemarie is given against all fluxes of the bloud; it is also good, especially the floures thereof, for all infirmities of the head and brain, proceeding of a cold and moist cause; for they dry the brain, quicken the senses and memorie, and strengthen the sinewie parts.

Serapio witnesseth, that Rosemarie is a remedie against the stuffing of the head, that cometh through coldnesses of the brain, if a garland thereof be put above the head whereof Abin Mesuai giveth testimonie. Discorides teacheth that it cureth him that hath the yellow jaundice, if it be boiled in water and drunk before exercise, and that after taking thereof of the patient bathe himself and drink wine.

The distilled water of the floures of Rosemarie being drunken at morning and evening first and last, taketh away the stench of the mouth and breath, and maketh it very sweet, if there be added thereto, to steepe or infuse to certain daies, a few Cloves, Mace, Cinnamon, and a little Anise seed.

The Arabians and other Physitions succeeding, do write that Rosemarie comforteth the brain and the memorie, the inward senses, and restoreth speech unto them that are possessed with the dumb palsie, especially the conserve of the floures and sugar, or any other confected with sugar, being taken every day fasting.

Tragus writeth, that Rosemarie is spice in the Germane Kitchens, and other cold countries. Further, he saith that the wine boiled with Rosemarie, and taken of women troubled by the mother, or the whites, helpeth them, the rather if they fast three or foure hours after.

The floures made up into plates with sugar after the manner of Sugar Roset and eaten, comfort the heart, and make it merry, quicken the spirits, and make them more lively.

The oile of Rosemarie chemically drawne, comforteth the cold, weake and feeble braine in most wonderfull manner.

The people of Thuingia do use the wilde Rosemarie to provoke the desired sicknesse.

Those of Marchia use to put it into their drinks the sooner to make their clients drunke, and also do put it into chests among clothes to preserve them from mothes or other vermine.

Rennaissance Garden Plant
'The Rosemarie is a plant of pleasant savour, which for the beautie and smell of it is set (at this day) in gardens. And the Gardners also in our time doe make divers seates, some like to benches, and other proper forms (as liketh them best to be delighted at) in their beds, running of length and of height.'
   The Proffitable Arte of Gardening
   Thomas Hyll, London, 1568

'Rosemarie, the cheefest beautie of Gardens and not to be wanted in the Kitchen . . . it is sette by women for their pleasure, to growe in sundry proportions, as in the fashion of a Cart, a Peacock, or such like thing as they fancie.'
> *Four Books of Husbandry*
> Barnabe Googe, 1577

'This common Rosemary is so well knowne through all our land, being in every woman's garden, that it were sufficient but to name it as an ornament among other sweete herbes and flowers in our Garden.'
> *Paradisus in Sole/Paradisus Terrestris*
> John Parkinson, London, 1629.

'*Gertrude Jekyll on Rosemary:* In the narrow border at the foot of the wall is a bush of *Raphiolepis ovata*, always to me an interesting shrub, with its thick, roundish, leathery leaves and white flower-clusters, also bushes of rosemary, some just filling the border, and some trained up the wall. Our Tudor ancestors were fond of rosemary-covered walls, and I have seen old bushes quite ten feet high on the garden walls of Italian monasteries. Among the rosemaries I always like, if possible, to 'tickle in' a China Rose or two, the tender pink of the rose seems to go so well with the dark but dull-surfaced rosemary'.
> *Wood and Garden*, 1899.

'I plant rosemary all over the garden, so pleasant is it to know that at every few steps one may draw the kindly branchlets through one's hand, and have the enjoyment of their incomparable incense; and I grow it against walls, so that the sun may draw out its inexhaustible sweetness to greet me as I pass; and early in March, before any other scented flower of evergreen is out, it gladdens me with the thick setting of pretty lavender-grey bloom crowding all along the leafy spikes.'

In the island of Capri, as elsewhere around the Mediterranean, rosemary is a common plant; but rambling over its rocky heights I found not unfrequently, besides the one of ordinary habit, a dwarf form, quite prostrate, pressing its woody stems and branches so tightly to any rock or stone that came in its way that it followed its form as closely as would a dwarf and clinging ivy.
Home and Garden, 1900

Rosemary in Two Seventeenth-Century Recipes for the Drink Mead

MEAD: An alcoholic liquor made by fermenting a mixture of honey and water.
The Shorter Oxford English Dictionary
Third Edition, 1972.

Queen Elizabeth's Recipe for Metheglin
One excellent receipt I will here recite: and it is of that which our renowned Queene of happie memorie did so well like, that she would every yeare have a vessell of it.

First gather a bushell of Sweetbriar-leaves, and a bushell of Tyme, halfe a bushell of Rosemarie, and a pecke of Bay-leaves. Seeth all these, being well washed in a furnace of faire water: let them boile the space of halfe an houre, or better: and then poure out all the water and herbes into a Vatt and let it stand till it be milk-warme; then straine the water from the herbes, take to everie six Gallons of water one Gallon of the finest Honie, and put it into the Boorne, and labour it together halfe and houre; then let it stand two daies, stirring it well twice or thrice a day.

Then take the liquor and boile it anew: and when it doth seeth, skim it as long as there remaineth drosse. When it is cleere put it into the Vatt as before, and there let it be cooled. You must then have in readinesse a Kieve of new Ale or Beere, which as soon as you have emptied, suddenly whelme it upside downe, and set it up in Barrels, tying at everie tap-hole, by a Pack-Thread a little bag of Cloves and Mace, to the value of an ounce. It must stand halfe a yeere before it be drunke.

Charles Butler,
The Feminine Monarchy, 1623

Hydromel as I made it weak for the Queen Mother
Take 18 quarts of spring-water, and one quart of honey; when the water is warm, put the honey into it. When it boileth up, skim it very well, and continue skimming it, as long as any scum will rise. Then put in one Race of Ginger (sliced in thin slices), four Cloves, and a little sprig of green Rosemary.

Let these boil in the liquor so long, till in all it have boiled one hour. Then set it to cool, till it be blood warm; and then put to it a spoonful of Ale-yest. When it is worked up, put it into a vessel of fit size; and after two or three days bottle it up. You may drink if after six weeks or two moneths. Thus was Hydromel made that I gave the Queen, which was exceedingly liked by everybody.

The Closet of the Eminently learned
Sir Kenelm Digby Kt. Opened 1668

The *Commentarii* of Pier Andrea Mattioli. Strasbourg, 1544.

ROSEMARY IN COOKING

John Philip de Linguamine in the fifteenth century describes rosemary as the customary condiment for salted meats.

'We will have . . . a good piece of beef, stuck with Rosemary!'
   'The Knight of the Burning Pestle'
   Beaumont & Fletcher, 1611

'Then the grim boar's head frown'd on high, Crested with Bays and rosemary.'
   'Marm'
   Scot, 1808

'The Ale, and the cider with rosemary in the bowl, were incomparable potations.'
   Eugene Aram
   Lord Lytton, 1831

To judge by the frequent references to lamb with rosemary, chicken with rosemary, veal with rosemary, which I note in the recent edition of the *Good Food Guide* as dishes which invariably draw enthusiastic comment, rosemary must be a high favourite in current English cookery. I can't say I share the taste to any extent. I have never cared for the way the Italians use it to flavour veal roasts, very often to excess. In Provence it often smothers the natural taste of lamb, and in the same region the little white goats' mild cheeses coated with rosemary spikes tend to taste of nothing else. (The alternative version, coated with *poivre d'ane* or wild savory is more to my taste, but is becoming rare.) Then, in France, there is the current mania for olives packed in jars of oil crammed to the corks with *herbes de Provence* – predominantly dried rosemary and thyme – and costing twice as much as olives which actually have their own taste. It's quite difficult to overpower the flavour of those little black olives, but rosemary does the trick. Sure, rosemary is for remembrance. I'd just rather it weren't for the remembrance of those little spiky leaves stuck in my throat.

It isn't that I have anything against rosemary as a plant. In the garden it smells delicious and looks enchanting. In my cooking it has little place, although I did learn a useful trick years ago in Capri when I caught sight of an old woman dipping a branch of rosemary in oil and gently brushing it over a fish she was roasting over a charcoal fire. An excellent notion.

'The Besprinkling of a Rosemary Branch'
Elizabeth David
The Herbal Review, 1980

Every plant should bear its part without being overpower'd by some Herb of stronger taste, so as to endanger the native Sapor and Vertue of the rest; but fall into their places like Notes in Music, in which should be nothing harsh or grating and though admitting some discords (to distinguish and illustrate the next) striking in the more sprightly and sometimes gentler notes reconcile all dissonances and melt them into an agreeable composition.'

Acetaria, A Discourse on Sallets
John Evelyn, London, 1699

The *Herbario Nuovo* of Castore Durante. Rome, 1585.

HERBS IN THE KITCHEN: The basic reason for using herbs in cooking is to add the flavour of the essential oil contained in each herb to the culinary process. The addition of this essential oil should enhance the flavour of each dish and may even be a key ingredient in making certain very bland foods more palatable: such as a herb vinaigrette with avocadoes, mint or caper sauce offered with old-fashioned mutton.

The pungency of a herb depends upon the volatile nature of the essential oil. In herbs that dry well: rosemary, thyme or sage, the essential oil is retained at almost its original strength, so that it is comparatively unimportant whether the herb is used fresh or dried. Equally, a long cooking process is necessary to extract these oils, so that rosemary, thyme and sage are admirable herbs to add to soups and stews, to roasted meats and other long cooking processes.

The herbs which have very volatile essential oils usually dry unsatisfactorily or change their flavour so much during the drying process as to seem to be a quite different plant. Such herbs are chives, parsley, basil and to a certain extent French tarragon. Since the fresh taste is so different from their dried form they should be added to a dish, either a couple of minutes before the end of the cooking, i.e. parsley for parsley sauce, or after the pot has left the stove, i.e. chives in almost all it uses.

Remember that 80 per cent of most herbs is water, so as a rule you will need to use five times as much of a fresh herb as in its dried form. Also keep in mind that herbs can usually only enhance a dish, but that they also very enormously in their strength, so be sparing with the French tarragon, but lavish with parsley; otherwise experiment to your heart's content, have fun, enjoy yourself, and your kitchen will be perhaps too full of friends and your dining table surrounded by admirers.

NOMEN HERBAE RHOSMARINI

The Herbal of Apuleius. Dioscorides and Apuleius, sixth/seventh century

SOME RECIPES WITH ROSEMARY: As rosemary is a herb which enjoys being baked by the sun its flavour does not change very much whether it is used fresh or dried. Its scent is strong and there is a whiff of pine about its flavour. In order to extract its essential oils it must be used at the beginning of any cooking process and the longer this process takes the more flavour of rosemary will be extracted.

It should never be used uncooked, and because of its spiky, woody nature it must be used with some care. If it is put uncrumbled straight into a dish it will result in your guests finding rather unattractive leaves and woody stalks when they come to eat the dish. It is therefore advisable in most cases to tie rosemary leaves up in a small muslin bag and remove them before presenting the dish at table, or removing the whole rosemary stalks before serving. An alternative is to grind dried rosemary into a powder in either a mortar or coffee grinder. A friend in West Somerset uses ground rosemary powder on joints of lamb and pork.

Rosemary Jelly
This jelly is ideal for serving with cold lamb and other cold meats.

1 pint rosemary leaves, pressed down
1 pint water
2 lb. cooking apples
1 lb. sugar
Juice of 1 lemon
2 tsp. powdered rosemary

Chop apples, including cores. Simmer rosemary in water for 5 minutes and remove. Add apples and boil for 30 minutes. Drain overnight through a jelly bag. Next day add 1 lb sugar for every pint of liquid. Boil steadily until the jelly sets, about 30 minutes. Skim and stir in the lemon juice and powdered rosemary.
   Pour into jars and seal when cool.

Rosemary with Chicken
Battery-fed or frozen chickens always need some extra treatment to cover the very bland taste of the flesh. This recipe takes advantage of considerable cooking time to bring out the essential oil of the rosemary.

1 tbs. rosemary
2 cloves garlic
¼ pint olive oil
2 tbs. butter
Seasoning: salt and pepper
1 small chicken, quartered
½ pint chicken stock
2 tbs. wine vinegar
Flour

Lightly coat the chicken with seasoned flour, fry lightly on all sides in the butter and oil, add crushed garlic, rosemary and seasoning and continue frying until browned all over. Stir in the stock and wine vinegar and cook in a moderate oven about 40 minutes, 340°F/Gas mark 4.
Serve with hot French bread and green salad.

Lamb Loaf
I do not think that pieces of lamb left over from a roast make a very good stew, but these remains can be minced very satisfactorily, as the following recipe shows.

2 lb. minced lamb
½ lb. bread crumbs
2 large beaten eggs
¼ pint stock or water
1 tbs. chopped parsley
¼ tsp. finely crumbled rosemary leaves
⅛ tsp. garlic powder or chopped garlic
¼ tsp. black pepper
1¾ tsp. salt
3 tbs. minced onion

Mix the lamb with the onion, chopped parsley, salt, pepper, eggs, garlic, breadcrumbs and stock or water, put into a loaf tin (9″ × 5″ × 3″) and bake 1 hour, 350°F. This loaf should be served with a rich home-made tomato sauce.

Shish Kebabs
Holiday memories of delicious juicy kebabs grilled over charcoal outside can be cruelly shattered when an attempt to reproduce them in England only seems to produce dried, tough pieces of meat on a skewer. The secret is to

marinate the meat for a sufficient length of time, and baste frequently during the cooking process.

1 tbs. mixed pickling spice
8 green pepper squares, 1½ in. each
8 wedges of firm tomatoes
8 mushroom caps
8 ¼ inch thick slices onion
2 lb. boneless leg of lamb
6 rosemary branches
1 tsp. each salt and poultry seasoning
10½ oz. beef bouillon
2 tbs. each cider vinegar and lemon juice
$^{1}/_{8}$ pint olive oil
½ tsp. each black pepper and onion powder
¼ tsp. garlic powder/chopped garlic

Place the bouillon, olive oil, vinegar, lemon juice, pepper, onion powder, garlic powder or garlic, salt and poultry seasoning into a pan, tie the pickling spice in a bag, boil all together for 2 minutes. Trim the fat from the lamb, cut the meat into cubes and marinade in the sauce together with the rosemary branches. Cool and refrigerate overnight. Next day put alternative pieces of lamb, green pepper squares, onion slices and mushroom caps on skewers and cook for 20-25 minutes over a cooling charcoal fire, using the rosemary branches to baste the kebabs occasionally with the marinade. Tomato wedges should be added after half of the cooking time.

Turkey Soufflé
There are always lots of bits and pieces left from a roast turkey and this recipe uses them quite effectively. The result is more of a baked egg dish than a towering soufflé.

12 oz. chopped turkey
1 tsp. lemon juice
½ tsp. salt
¼ tsp. finely crumbled rosemary leaves
Good pinch of black pepper
4 large eggs, separated
3 tbs. butter
3 tbs. flour
$1/8$ pint turkey stock and thin cream or milk

Blend the flour and butter over gentle heat, cook ½ minute. Remove from heat and stir in the milk or cream and stock, cook over a low heat until smooth, add beaten egg yolks and finally all the other ingredients except the egg whites, which must be beaten until stiff. Fold them into the mixture and turn into a 2-pint soufflé dish, buttered only on the bottom. Put the dish in a pan of hot water and place in a slow oven 325°F. for 1½ hours, or until a testing skewer comes out clean.

Veal and Ham Casserole
Veal and ham go excellently together and the following dish can be very useful as a main course for a picnic in the summer.

2 lb. boneless shoulder of veal
¼ tsp. each minced garlic and minced onion
½ tsp. finely crumbled rosemary leaves
1 lb. diced cooked ham
1 tin of potatoes
2 tbs. butter
1 tsp. salt
4 tbs. flour
$1/8$ pint milk
1½ pints water

Cut veal in 1 inch cubes and brown in butter, add garlic, onion, water, salt and rosemary. Cover, bring to boiling point, reduce heat and simmer 30 minutes. Blend flour with milk to a smooth paste, add some of the veal stock and add to the meat. Stir in the ham and cook 5 minutes. Then, cook uncovered in a moderate oven for 30 minutes. Cool. Refrigerate in a 2-quart container and just before serving put the potatoes around the edge of the dish.

Fried Parsnips
Since we have to live with root vegetables for six months of the year, here is a way of making parsnips rather more interesting.

1 tsp. finely crumbled rosemary leaves
¼ lb. breadcrumbs
2 large beaten eggs
1 lb. parsnips
$1/8$ pint fat or oil for frying
1½ tsp. salt
½ inch boiling water

Slice parsnips lengthwise $1/8$ inch thick and cook for about 12 minutes in boiling salted water. Remove, dip into beaten eggs and then breadcrumbs mixed with rosemary and a little salt. Fry on both sides until brown.

Rosemary with Oranges
In the seventeenth century rosemary was used a great deal as a flavouring for desserts. Here is a simple modern recipe, but do remember to remove the sprigs of rosemary after the syrup has been made.

3 6-in. sprigs rosemary
8 oz. honey
6 oranges
¾ pint water

Bring the rosemary, water and honey slowly to the boil, then boil fast for 5 minutes. Cool. Peel the oranges and cut away all the pith and remove all pips. Slice very thinly and over them strain the cooled syrup. Chill.

Rosemary Fruit Cup
Different cool drinks on summer days are always appreciated. This one has a refreshing tang. For a final touch add rosemary flowers frozen in ice cubes just before serving.

1 small handful top sprigs of rosemary
1 can concentrated orange juice
2 cans water for juice
¼ pint water
1 tbs. honey
1 pint ginger ale

Simmer the rosemary sprigs in the ¼ pint water and honey for 5 minutes. Cool. Strain into a large jug, pour over the chilled orange juice and ginger ale and add ice cubes.

Gin and Pineapple Punch
Before lunch on Sunday is the time when people need a reviving and refreshing drink with a slight kick. This recipe is admirable, particularly if it is preceding brunch rather than the traditional English lunch.

½ pint lemon juice
1 bottle of gin
2 tbs. sugar
Dash salt
2 20-oz cans pineapple juice
2½ tsp. rosemary leaves
Whole cloves and fresh lemon slices

Into a 2-quart saucepan put the rosemary leaves and ½ cup of pineapple juice, bring to the boil and then cool. Leave for 5 minutes. Strain out rosemary leaves and add the other ingredients, reserving the lemon slices stuck with cloves for decoration. Pour into punch bowl over ice.

Rosemary Flowers in Ice Cubes
Freeze the small blue flowers of rosemary in ice cubes and add to Fruit Cup.

Crystallised Rosemary Flowers
Ready-made cake decorations are not very attractive. Crystallised rosemary flowers are easy to make and keep well.

Paint the flowers with the white of 1 egg lightly mixed with 1 tbs. water. Dry in a cool oven or airing cupboard. Dust with caster sugar and store in a tin or jar between layers of waxed paper.

OTHER USES OF ROSEMARY: Milled dried rosemary was often used as a substitute for expensive incense.

Colonial Americans in the eighteenth century thought that a rosemary rinse preserved not only the colour in brown and black hair, but also the curl.

In herbal medicine today rosemary is prescribed as a tonic, astringent, diaphoretic – property of promoting sweating; it is also an excellent stomachic and nervine, and for curing cases of headache, colic, cold and even nervous depression. An infusion combined with borax makes a good hair wash and will prevent, allegedly, premature baldness.

Oil of Rosemary, which is extracted from the leaves of the plant, has been valued for centuries and it is still listed in the United States Pharmacopoeia; the oil is also used in verterinary medicine.

The oil from this herb is still used in many cosmetic preparations for both skin and hair. It is an ingredient of the finest French Eau-de-Cologne. Here is an eighteenth-century English recipe for the famous 'Hungary Water' or 'Queen of Hungary Water', which was devised in the thirteenth century by a hermit to cure Queen Elizabeth of Hungary who was suffering from a paralysis; a twentieth-century variation is being offered in department stores in London and New York at the moment, but I doubt somehow the manufacturer uses the following recipe:

> 'Take to every *gallon of Brandy*, or clean Spirits, one handful of Rosemary, one handful of Lavender. I suppose the handfuls to be about a Foot Long a-piece; and these Herbs must be cut in Pieces about an inch long. Put these to infuse in the Spirits and with them about one handful of Myrtle, cut as before. When this has stood three days, distil it, and you will have the finest Hungary-Water that can be. It has been said that Rosemary flowers are better than the Stalks; but they give a faintness to the Water, and should not be used, because they have a quite different smell from the Rosemary, nor should the Flowers of Myrtle be used in lieu of the Myrtle, for they have a scent ungrateful, and not at all like the Myrtle!
> R. Bradley
> *The Country Housewife and Lady's Director*, 1732

Home-made Rosemary Cosmetics

Rosemary Water

Barely cover the rosemary with cold water and simmer for 5 minutes. Cool strain and bottle.

Rosemary Astringent Lotion

7 tbs. rosemary water
5 tbs. orange flower water
1 tbs. witch hazel
½ tsp. powdered borax

Put the rosemary and borax in a bowl and stand over hot water. Heat gently and stir until the borax has dissolved. Cool and add to the witch hazel and orange flower water; then pour into screw cap bottles.

Rosemary Cold Cream

3 fl. oz. almond oil
½ oz. white wax
¼ tsp. powdered borax
3 tbs. rosemary water

Heat the oil and wax gently in a bowl over hot water until melted. Warm the rosemary water and stir into it the borax until dissolved. Gradually add to the wax and oil, beating thoroughly all the time. Remove from heat and continue beating until quite smooth. Cool and turn into small pots. Use within 3 weeks.

Rosemary Hair Tonic

Cover the rosemary with cold water, simmer 15 minutes. Strain, cool and pour into screw cap bottles.

> 'Carry powder of the flower about thee, to make thee merry, glad, gracious, and well-beloved of all men. . . . Lay the flowers on thy bed to keepe thee free from all evill dreames. . . . To comfort the heart, seethe rosemary and the flowers with Rose water, and drinke it. The conserve of the flowers comforteth the heart marvelously. To preserve thy youth make a box of the wood and smell to it.
> *The Garden of Health*
> William Langham, 1579.

Codex Vindobonensis. Dioscorides, 512 A.D.

De Historia Stirpium. Leonhard Fuchs. Basel, 1542

SOURCES, AUTHORITIES AND TITLES FOR FURTHER READING

Amherst, Alicia
A History of Gardening in England.
Quaritch. London, 1895.

Anderson, Frank J.
An Illustrated History of the Herbals.
Columbia University Press. New York, 1977.

Arber, Agnes
Herbals: Their Origin and Evolution.
Cambridge University Press, 1912.

Beard, James
American Cookery.
Little, Brown & Co. Boston, 1972.

Beck, Bertholle and *Child*
Mastering the Art of French Cooking.
Knopf. New York, 1964.

Bianchini F. and *F. Corbetta*
The Kindly Fruits.
Cassell. London, 1977.

Boxer, Arabella and *Phillipa Back*
The Herb Book.
Octopus. London, 1980.

Brownlow, Margaret
Herbs and the Fragrant Garden.
Darton, Longman and Todd. London, 1963.

Clarkson, Rosetta E.
The Golden Age of Herbs and Herbalists.
Dover. New York, 1972.

Crockett, James Underwood and *Ogden Tanner*
Herbs from Time-Life Encyclopedia of Gardening.
Alexandria, Virginia, 1977.

David, Elizabeth
French Country Cooking.
Penguin Books. London, 1959.

David, Elizabeth
Spices, Salt and Aromatics in the English Kitchen
Penguin Books. London, 1970.

Garland, Sarah
The Herb and Spice Book.
Frances Lincoln Ltd. London, 1979.

Genders, Roy
The Complete Book of Herbs and Herb Growing
Ward Lock Ltd. London, 1980.

Gerard, John
The Herball or General History of Plants.
London, 1633.

Gregg, Richard and *Helen Philbrick*
Companion Plants and How to Use Them.
Robinson & Watkins. London, 1966.

Grieve, Mrs M.
A Modern Herbal: Edited and Introduced by
Mrs C. F. Leyel.
Cape. London, 1931. Reprinted 1974.

Hemphill, Rosemary
Herbs for All Seasons.
Penguin Books. London, 1975.

Henrey, Blanche
British Botanical and Horticultural Literature before 1800.
OUP, 1975.

Hibberd, Shirley
The Amateur's Kitchen Garden.
W. H. and L. Collingridge. London, 1893.

Jekyll, Gertrude
Wood and Garden.
Longmans, Green & Co. London, 1899.

Jekyll, Gertrude
Home and Garden.
Longmans, Green & Co. London, 1900.

Lehane, Brendan
The Power of Plants.
John Murray. London, 1977.

Leyel, Mrs C. F.
The Magic of Herbs.
Jonathan Cape. London, 1926.

Loewenfeld and *Back*
The Complete Book of Herbs and Spices.
David & Charles. Newton Abbot, Devon, 1974.

Loewenfeld, Claire
Herb Gardening.
Faber and Faber. London, 1964.

Lowinsky, Ruth and *Thomas*
Lovely Food - A Cookery Notebook.
The Nonesuch Press. London, 1931.

Morgenthau Fox, Helen
Gardening with Herbs for Flavor and Fragrance.
Dover Publications. New York, 1933.

Northcote, Lady Rosalind
The Book of Herbs.
The Bodley Head. London, 1903

Robinson, William
The English Flower Garden.
John Murray. London, 1893.

Rohde, Eleanor Sinclair
The Old English Herbals
Longmans, Green & Co. London, 1922.

Rohde, Eleanor Sinclair
Shakespeare's Wild Flowers, Fairy Lore, Gardens, Herbs, Gatherers of Simples and Bee Lore.
The Medici Society. London.

Rohde, Eleanor Sinclair
A Garden of Herbs.
P. E. Warner & Medici Society. London.

Rohde, Eleanor Sinclair
The Old World Pleasaunce.
Herbert Jenkins. London, 1925.

Rombauer and *Becker*
The Joy of Cooking.
Bobbs, Merrill. New York, 1931.

Root, Waverley
Food.
Simon and Schuster. New York, 1980

Sackville-West, Vita
Garden Book.
Michael Joseph. London, 1968.

Sanecki, Kay N.
The Complete Book of Herbs.
Macdonald and Jane's. London, 1974.

Simmons, Adelma Grenier
Herb Gardening in Five Seasons.
Hawthorn Books. New York, 1964.

Simmons, Adelma Grenier
Herbs to Grow Indoors.
Hawthorn Books. New York, 1969.

Stobart, Tom
Herbs, Spices and Flavourings.
David & Charles. Newton Abbot, Devon, 1970.

Stuart, Malcolm, Ed.
The Encyclopedia of Herbs and Herbalism.
Orbis Publishing. London, 1979.

Woodward, Marcus
Leaves from Gerard's Herball.
Houghton Mifflin. Boston, 1931.

Larousse Gastronomique.
Hamlyn. London, 1961.

Oxford English Dictionary.
Oxford University Press. Oxford, 1979.

The Royal Horticultural Society. Dictionary of Gardening.
Oxford, 1951.

The Wisley Handbook of Culinary Herbs.
Royal Horticultural Society. London, 1974.

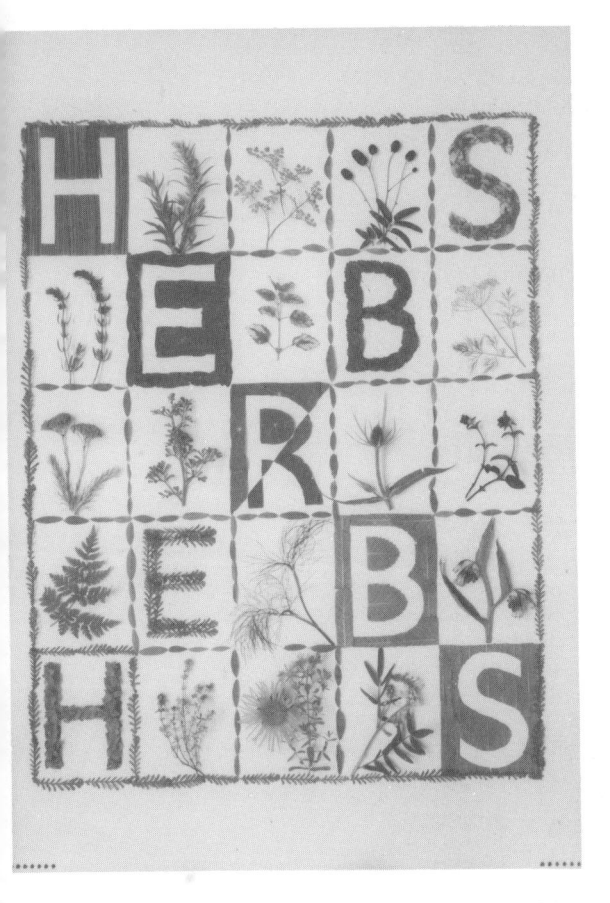

The Herb Society Poster. Image by Tessa Traeger. Design by Terry Stratton. Copies available from The Society

Publications from The Herb Society include:

In Praise of Parsley £1.50
A Multitude Mints £1.50
The Romance of Rosemary £1.50
In Celebration of Chives £1.50
Growing Herbs £0.95
Pomanders, Washballs and Other Scented Articles £0.95
Herbal Hair Colouring £0.95
A Guide to Spices £0.95
The Herb Society Poster £1.50 (plus 25p P & P)

Please include 25p postage per book with your order. Further details from The Secretary, The Herb Society, 34 Boscobel Place, London SW1.

Juniper Press Publications include:

The Little Brown Cook Books Series
Pot-pourri From Your Garden
Pressed Flowers
Country Cooking: Fruit Recipes
Country Cooking: Mushroom Recipes
Country Cooking: Honey Recipes
Country Cooking: Herb Recipes

For a complete free catalogue and order form write to:
The Juniper Press,
P.O. Box 23,
Winchester,
Hants.
SO23 9TP.